Prepare for Scholarship Money

What it Takes to Help Receive

Scholarships and Student Aid

By

Jody Duffey

Table of Content

First printing 2015

Same Middle Name Publishing Company

Introduction

I wrote this to help high school students have a chance to receive scholarships and grants. Scholarship money helps to pay for most post high school education: colleges, universities and trade schools. Most scholarships are based on your accomplishments during your high school years. I show you options on how to fulfill these achievements. To do this you need to have volunteer hours, leadership skills, committee titles, a resume and more. You will need to start acquiring hours and titles between the time you have completed eighth grade and December of your high school year. After you graduate from eighth grade you are considered to be in high school, so summer counts. Most college and scholarship applications are sent in December or January of your senior year. This is the time period you need to be working on your achievements. What you do in high school determines which college will accept you and what financial aid you will receive.

This book contains suggestions on how be accepted into advanced education institutions and "stand out" for scholarships and grants' committees. The following information does not guarantee that you will be accepted into the university of your choice or receive the scholarships or grants you are applying for, but it will put you a step in front of most high school graduates. In this book, college and university are interchangeable. Either term can also stand for trade school. In addition feminine and masculine pronouns are interchanged in an effort to keep the reading smoother.

Chapter 1 WHAT IF?????

- What if you need money for college?

- What if you are not lower income, minority, athletic, top of the class, or talented?

- What if you do not want to part with your money or incur a large debt?

- What if you need help getting into a selective school?

- What if the military is not for you?

- What if you want to stand out for a military academy?

If any of the above applies to you, I can give you tips for success. I can help you stand out from other applicants. It will teach you how to look polished. Most important of all I will show you the value of volunteering or community service.

This book will help you to qualify, complete and document community service for a scholarship. This is hard work, but it is also fun.

This book will teach you how:

- To volunteer effectively

- To run for office positions in clubs

- To volunteer on a national level

- To initiate an independent volunteer event

- To write a great resume

- To interview with confidence

- To record information and keep track of your volunteer work

Chapter 2 GETTING STARTED

After you are promoted from eighth grade you are considered a high school student! This is the time to start preparing for college--to start thinking of what you want to do. It is also a time to begin thinking of different clubs and volunteer work to get an idea of what you like. To look good on a scholarship or college application, **volunteer or community service hours are crucial!**

Volunteer Hours

To volunteer means to help out when you are not obligated to do so. You need to accumulate many volunteer hours- more than most school require for Honor Society. You should try for 300 hours. It sounds like a huge number, but if you pace yourself, it is attainable. This is over a four year period. This is an accumulation of all your volunteer hours including volunteer work for groups to which you already belong. Summer is a good time to do some heavy volunteering.

For example if you volunteer:

1.5 (hrs. a wk.) **X 52** (wks.)= **78** (volunteer hours)

1.5 X 52 = 78   That is 78 (hrs. per year.)

78 X 4= 312   That is 78 (hrs. a year) X 4 (yrs.) = 312

Remember that is one and a half hours a week times fifty-two weeks in a year times four years. You will find that it is much easier to accumulate many hours at one time doing one big activity, but always keep close count of your hours to make sure you are on track.

Try to have the following number of accumulated hours.

Total by May of freshman year-- 78 hours

Total by May of sophomore year--156 hours

Total by May of junior year-- 234 hours

Total by December of senior year-- 312

If you have a semester with very hard classes, you should go light on volunteer activities. Stay active in your clubs. If you have an easy semester, take on an independent project. The summer or spring or winter breaks are a good time for collecting extra volunteer hours so you can keep on track.

Volunteering makes you feel good about yourself and makes you more confident. It opens you up too new experiences and you might make some friends along the way. It gives scholarship judges and college admission representatives a chance to see another side of you.

CHAPTER 3 SETTING UP AN ACHIEVEMENT BOOK

Your achievement book or notebook will become your history of all your accomplishments, achievements and awards. While other students will be digging through old papers and trying to remember what they have done in their sophomore year of high school, you will have it all organized in a neat three ring binder. You will also have signed verification of your work. This will help you with college admissions as well as possibly opening doors for scholarships. **Think of this book as potentially earning you college money..** It will also help you to get your foot in the door at a university. This can help you fill out college and scholarship application with confidence. **Important hint: Only show people copies of the book. Keep the original book in a safe place**.

Most college scholarship applications ask for activities, clubs, offices held, community involvement awards, and a work resume. By the time you are a senior, your mind might be a blur of what happened in ninth grade. By keeping track of what you have done, you will be prepared, organized and steps ahead of the other students.

Purchase list:

- 3 ring binders- at least two
- Pocket sheet protectors–medium weight suggested
- Pocket divider
- Wall calendar or digital calendar
- Small calendar you can keep with you- a hard copy
- Colored felt pens (Easier to write on wall calendar)
- Thank you notes-plain and tasteful stationary-simple with your name or initials
- Postage stamps
- Box to store
- Recording device- could be on a phone
- Digital Camera or camera phone

Set up two achievement books. One will be good for several years. When you need to start showing it to counselors, schools or use it for applications, a copy is nice bonus. You can set up one book as the original and copy it or set up two books from the start. Buy a solid three ring binder a couple of inches deep. Purchase a binder with a clear front cover pocket where you can change the cover for different occasions. Choose a color you like. You can slide a cover page in the front and change it as you wish. **Do not ever let the original out of your home; only show copies.** This book is too valuable to trust with anyone outside the safety of your home.

Make sure you have a safe cover or blank front on your copy if you need to show it to a counselor, college or scholarship representative. If you are taking a copy of the book you may want a cover page with your name or an interesting photo of you and one of your interests.

Above all, do not decorate your notebook with any type of gang symbols, references to sex, alcohol, or drugs. Even if it is hidden, your evaluator might be only a few years older than you and recognize something tasteless.

Pocket sheet protectors of medium weight are available at discount and office supply stores. Top loading or side loading is a matter of personal preference.

<u>Dividers</u>

Label the dividers:

- Resume

- Transcript

- Awards and Honors

- Volunteer

- Clubs and Committees

- Letters

- Photography

- Others: These can be the name of a club or organization that you participate, or an individual sporting event in which you excel. You will need a separate category for this.

Put all your papers in your binder in pocket sheet protectors. It looks better than having holes punched into the paper. It will also protect papers from wear. They will be fresh when you need to copy them and more valuable to you later.

Resume

This will be your high school and work resume combined. This is a combination of your work, awards clubs and skills. See explanation of how to write a resume in chapter ten —"Writing a Strong Resume."

Transcript

Keep all official records of your grades and classes taken. Be sure to list any AP (Advance Placement) or college credit classes you have taken. Keep **all** your report cards.

Awards and Honors

Any award or honor you receive from any organization is important. For example: clubs, scouts, religious institutions, and letters of thanks for volunteer work. If you do work for an organization and have not documented your hours, ask them for a letter for your college file. Most organizations are glad to send you a letter. If you want to frame a certificate, award or letter make sure you photocopy it first and put the copy of the original in your book. If the certificate has pretty colors, spend the extra money for a color photocopy.

Volunteer

Keep all of your volunteer work hours documented and save pamphlets and news articles about your volunteer causes. Also keep any program, news article, pamphlet, as advertisement for your events.

Committees Clubs

Include information on school clubs and clubs out of school. For example: scouts or community volunteering. Have a separate category if one club is very involved. Keep information on your activities on scouting, Future Farmers of America, debate team, or sport team. News articles of an event you participated and programs from events also look good in your binder.

Letters

Keep all letters of recommendation along with correspondence or congratulation letters. You may receive these from organizations you have worked for such or from a politician or influential people that know you. Keep letters from employers and letters of thanks from organizations that you have helped.

Photographs

If you can, buy some pages that the photos slide in with three holes that fit into your notebook. If not, mount the photo on acid free paper and put it in the pocket sheet protectors. You can also put news clipping here if you wish. Laminating helps to preserve newspaper clippings or scan and save.

Others Sections

You can always add a divider on your own. Sports, photographs of animals you raised, science projects, and debate transcripts are good. Whatever you think is important, keep! If you feel like a pack rat, remember it is always easier to thin out your book than to try to recreate a letter, award, or photo later. When in doubt, keep it. You might even need a back-up box. You can buy boxes in all shapes and sizes at container stores, office supply, craft and discount stores. A shoebox also works.

CHAPTER 4 SIZING UP YOUR TALENTS

Volunteer

Everyone has talents, interests or natural gifts. All volunteer activities are going to cost in money, transportation and time. The time can be as frequent as you want. It may involve having a parent or friend drive you somewhere. Check to see if you can find support from family members or trusted friends. Remind them it may lead to scholarships for you or at least you're becoming a better person. Everyone has talents, interests or natural gifts. You might meet someone with influence that has seen your work and could write a letter of recommendation. Be prepared for a criminal background check for anything involving children or seniors.

* Always check in advance if your work or donations will be accepted and appreciated.

* Never volunteer at a place where your personal safety is in danger.

* Never work alone with children, handicapped people, or seniors where there could be any question or false charges of abuse or molestation. If you do work with children, handicapped people, or seniors have an adult you trust in viewing area at all times.

Note

If you are on a committee or doing an event out of town, your traveling time will count as volunteer hours. Shopping for supplies for your projects and your time publicizing your event counts as volunteer hours.

Do you like the nature, animals or gardening?

Volunteer at a garden in a nursing home at a park. You might also work at a pet shelter. Check if you can beautify your city or neighborhood by talking to your city council or head of the parks in your area. Plant trees. Have people buy trees in honor or memory of a loved one. Start a victory garden and have the food go to a soup kitchen. You may also involve a day care in the teaching of farming. Many city kids have not seen crops grow. A nursing home or school may want to have a garden of vegetables, flowers or plants. A place of worship may want a meditation garden.

Do you like physical activity?

Do you want to build muscles? Do you need more exercise? Can you build things? Food banks need help loading and unloading food. Check with the veteran organizations or senior centers to see if you can build ramps or handrails for them if you have carpentry skills. Remember to check for city codes or if permits are required.

Do you sew, knit or crochet?

Nursing homes need lap robes and bibs. Check to see if they are welcome before making them. They may request a size or pattern. Charity Hospitals might need baby blankets or knit hats for newborns. Patterns have been designed for clutter holders to tuck under the mattress to hold TV remotes, glasses, tissues, etc. Check to see if homeless shelters or cancer units would welcome hand knit hats. Every hour of knitting crocheting or sewing, counts along with delivering the item. Ask if they have a pattern. If not, show a sample of yours to see if it is acceptable.

Are you good at writing?

Write the history of a senior citizen. Check with senior apartments, nursing homes, or the VA hospital to find people who have stories to tell. Their story will be a treasure to family members and will make the seniors feel important. The cost can be as minimal as paper and a folder. You can also save their stories by putting the work on a computer and include scanned photographs. Go to the veteran hospital, nursing home, senior apartments and collect stories. **Remember do not meet in their apartment or room. Meet in a community room.**

Are you good with computers?

Volunteer to teach at a library, community center, AARP or nursing home. If you belong to a place of worship, volunteer to hold a computer class. The simple use of the Internet opens up the world to people. Can you scan items of a group or place of worship electronically? Copies could also be sold as a fundraiser.

Are you good with children?

Ask a librarian they have a program where you could read to little kids? Check to see if you can help a scout leader or be an assistant? Are you good at a sport? Help coach a little league team.

Are you good with at a subject or want to be a teacher?

Maybe you could can start a before or after school tutoring class. You could also teach a class at an assisted living center or senior apartment. You might organize a group to read a play together.

Can you organize?

Check to see if any charity, nonprofit or political organization could use your office skills such as filing and data entry?

Can you sing or play an instrument?

Perform at a daycare or nursing home. Remember to play to the audience. Some old people want to hear songs from their youth. Kids like fun, silly songs. Remember, keep the songs clean.

Do you know more than one language?

Help translate at a volunteer shop or community center. See might also see if you could tutor.

Do you like politics?

Politicians need people to make phone calls, stuff envelopes and perform many other chores. Perhaps you could have a voter registration drive. Keep track of how many people take forms. Get to know the candidates if it is an election year. Hint: If you can choose between politicians, chose the one that looks like he will win or the one that went to the college you are applying. They might help with a letter of recommendation or help you get a foot in the door later. Do not volunteer for politicians that have views in contrast from what you believe. This can become an embarrassment that you worked for them.

Do you enjoy party organizing?

Help set up parties for charitable events. Keep a journal of the theme, budget and photographs. Keep detailed photographs of any item you designed such as centerpieces, place cards, or invitations.

Do you consider yourself a cook?

Sell baked goods for a cause. Check with health board in the city or county so you will comply with their health and food laws.

Do you know what career you want to pursue?

If so, what skills are needed for that career? What can you do now to learn more and become more experienced in that field? If you are interested in a medical career, volunteer at a hospital. If you are interested in a science career, see if a museum matches your interest.

Are you artistic?

Volunteer to paint walls in a hospital, senior center, nursing home, or lower income day care. Some hardware stores have mismatched paint that you can get cheaply. You might ask for the paint to be donated since it is going for a cause. Make an appointment with the store manager and have a formal letter with your request. Include what supplies you need and what charity organization or lower income place is benefiting from your work. Have a sponsor-approved letter supporting your project to show to the hardware or paint store.

Do you Cheer or dance?

Teach young students to cheer. Have this school sponsored. If not, check with the YMCA or place of worship and see if can sponsor your class. If you are on a cheer team get the team sponsors' approval. Charge a fee and have it go to a good cause. Ask an adult to help you. This is part of the never being alone with a child rule. Managing a cheer or dance event shows organizational skills. Look into any insurance liability protection that the school or YMCA could cover.

Do you have a flair for fashion?

Have a fashion show fundraiser. Many churches or nursing homes will let you have a fashion show around Mother's Day, or have a prom fashion show. See if a charity clothing store will let you use their clothes. Try a small independent one first. Then you are promoting two organizations at once. You would also be promoting the thrift store. Collect clothing and jewelry for a lower income high schools or shelters. You could collect formal clothes for school prom, professional clothes for working women, or maternity and baby clothes and miscellaneous baby items.

Do you enjoy scrap booking?

Help organize a scrapbook for a club, place of worship, or group of senior citizens. Use photocopies if they do not want to use originals. Do not take the scrapbook home. This way you are not responsible if irreplaceable items get lost. Leave the scrapbook with a trusted individual.

Do you know what cause you stand for?

What cause do you believe in? Do you or a relative have an illness? Was your parent, grandparent, or other relative a veteran? Was your mom a single mother? Has your family overcome a hardship? Many of scholarship and college applications ask who inspired you, what obstacles' you have overcome and what did you learn from the experience.

Example:

My uncle had diabetes and I organized a fun run team in his honor.

Example:

My grandfather is a veteran, so I had a book drive for the VA hospital.

Example:

You might have a relative that overcame hardships. You want to make life a little better for someone with similar difficulties. This is great for an inspirational essay. You could write how a special person inspired you to do something for a cause. Make sure you have someone to accept what you collect before you put any substantial time into the event.

Put your proposal in writing and submit it to the people in charge of the event. Keep track of the number of people that helped and the amount of money raised if it is impressive. Remember while you are trying to raise money for an organization, you are also promoting yourself. Writing the letter or proposal also counts as volunteer time you should record.

Example:

Record Keeping:

I had a garage sale with 153 donors; the money went to Texas Children's Hospital for leukemia research.

If a person only donated one item, he counts as a contributor. If you raised a large amount, note the dollar amount on your resume or applications.

Example

Organized garage sale for Leukemia Society with 153 contributors raising $834.

Another example for an application letter: I was team captain and leader of a team for the Susan G. Komen Race for the Cure. I lead a team of seventeen, and we collected pledges totaling $850.00.

If you are volunteering by yourself, you can help with organizing, setting up booths, or water breaks for runs or bike races. This all counts as volunteer hours.

Chapter 5 JOINING CLUBS and ORAGINIZATIONS

When you work with an organization, if possible publicize and photograph your fundraiser or volunteer work. Contact a newspaper, your parent's employer's magazine or a place of worship's publication to see if they will publish your information.

Committee

Committee work means being a person or part of a group of persons elected or appointed to perform some service or function, as to investigate, report on, or act upon a particular matter.

Holding a position on committee for a nonprofit or charitable organization earns you volunteer hours. Meetings count as volunteer time. One meeting a month should cover several of your volunteer hours. If you join a club in the community or at school that has weekly meetings, they do not count as volunteer hours. When the meetings are about an upcoming charity event such as a fundraiser, the hours count. A book club does not count as charitable work. When your book club has a used book drive for soldiers, nursing home, the hours count as charitable volunteer hours.

Holding a Title on a Committee

A title can be president, representative, secretary, treasurer, historian, photographer, team captain, fundraiser, or web site designer. This title can be in a school club, religious group, scout or an organization you belong to out of school. If they do not have a historian or photographer or other position that interests you, create or volunteer for the title. Participate in a few committees or clubs in or out of school in your freshman year to find out which ones you enjoy. Narrow your involvement to two or three that meet often to keep it manageable. If one meets less often, it is easy to take on extra responsibilities in this organization. Then run or volunteer for a titled position. Check if they are connected to a larger organization, city, regional or state and volunteer to be their representative to the higher organization.

School Clubs

Organize a fundraiser for a need that relates to your club. See if there is a charity walk, bike ride, or toy drive that you can lead for your club. For example: If you are in R.O.T.C., participate in the Marines Toys for Tots by organizing a toy drive in your community. For better publicity, wear your R.O.T.C. uniform when you take in the donations and have a photograph taken.

Scouts

Scout troops are usually small and it is easy to hold a position in your troop. If one is not available for you, create a position such as historian, treasurer, or secretary. Try to organize an event that will help a cause. Try to be elected to something that could lead to a higher lever such as city, state or national representative. Being an Eagle Scout or earning a similar award looks good and the hours for the award can be added to your total accumulated hours of volunteer work.

Worship

Most places of worship have conferences that are at the county, regional or state level. Try to be selected as a youth representative and go to a conference. You might ask for donations to help with your travel expenses. Some scholarships ask what local, state or national level titles you have held in an organization. If you do not have a youth representative, create the position. Represent your place of worship. This could be a weekend vacation for your family and a chance for you to pick up titles and volunteer hours. If the church is sending a group already, see if you can join them. This is also an opportunity to meet people that may help you later.

Chapter 6 VOLUNTEERING INDEPENDENTLY

Individual Charitable Event

This means you do something for the community on your own. You need to initiate a charitable drive or fund raising event by yourself. This shows leadership and impresses scholarship judges and college admission officers. In today's world there is always some type of disaster or event that needs money, clothing, blankets, books, or household goods. This can be a spur of the moment cause. Collect clothing, household goods, and food. Example: school supplies for a neighborhood tragedy such as an apartment fire, flood, tornado or other need.

National Level

This could be a charity on a national level such as cancer, diabetes, Multiple Sclerosis races, telethons, veteran's organizations or even Toys for Tots. Example of volunteering on a national level can be runs, walks or bike rides, phone telethons, national toy or clothing drives, or a garage sale with the money going to a national cause.

Always find some organization that will accept the donation you collected for them. Always offer a receipt for the item donated. Find a cause to donate. Ask a local celebrity, radio or TV or senator, congressman for a donation. To earn money hold events such as garage sales, theater performances, dinners or whatever with the fund going to the disaster or need. Just make sure you have volunteered to lead the event and that you first have someone to accept what you collect before you put any time into the event.

An independent project shows strong leadership skills. Start a project on your own. Decide what you want to do and first see if someone wants your donation. After an organization is willing to take your donation of items or cash write a plan. In this proposal write the steps you will be taking from start to finish on how you will accomplish your goal. This will also give you a plan to show a teacher, club or place of worship to help you get a sponsor. If you cannot find a sponsor continue with your idea if you think it is a project that is needed and one you can handle. It is better to take on a small task that you can accomplish than a larger one that you will not be able to complete. Keep track of your time on your time log. Record all hours spent writing the proposal, talking and publicizing the event, doing the event and making the donation. This is a good time to take photos. Try and get them in a newspaper after you have completed the project. Contact the newspaper in advance to publicize the event if it is a garage sale or something else that involves your community. See if stores, restaurants, or banks will let you post your event or put flyers in their window

Put your proposal in writing and submit it to the people in charge of the event. Keep track of the number of people that help and the amount of money raised if it is impressive. Remember while you are trying to raise money for an organization, you are also promoting yourself. Writing the letter or proposal also counts as volunteer time you should record.

Record Keeping Example

I had a garage sale with 153 donors; the money went to Texas Children's Hospital for leukemia research.

If you are volunteering by yourself, you can help with organizing, setting up booths, or water breaks for runs or bike races. This all counts as volunteer hours.

Writing your independent volunteer plan for a donation, include

- What is your cause?

- What you are collecting?

- Who acceptance of your donation?

- How will you solicit donations?

- Will you need collection boxes?

- What is your time span of your collection?

- How will you pick up the items?

- Who is the person that is receiving them? Make an appointment to deliver the items

Most people have too much clutter in their homes. Too many do dads, too many books. People keep them but are willing to give them to a worthy cause. It is easier to get most people to donate something they no longer need than to donate money.

Detail on things to collect and donate

Books

Books for veterans

Books for prisons

Books for soldiers

Books for nursing homes

Books for homeless shelter

Books for lower income housing

Books for low-income day care

If they do not have a library ask if you can start one. If you cannot get a bookshelf donated consider it a good investment, or get cinder blocks and wood and build a bookshelf. They may accept the books without a bookshelf. This is a great photo op and news items.

Pet shelters

Towels and rugs for animal shelters

Cleaning products

Pet collars and leashes

New pet toys

Newspaper

First check if they have a list of items that they will accept.

Garage Sale items

People are willing to donate usable items for a cause. Have a garage sale for a cause you believe. Use your drive way or a friend's. Ask a local business if you can use their parking lot. Good for both of you. Draws people to their business. Have a silent auction for your cause. You are going to have to find a place to have the auction. Most garage sells do better the Saturday and after the first or 15th of the month which is most people's payday.

If you have a successful garage sale and donate the money, you have completed an event for a national organization.

National Toy or Clothing Drives

Each holiday season several national organizations make a plea to the public for toys or clothing to help needy families. Lots of people will buy one or more gifts to donate to a needy child. Hold a collection site and call friends and family for donations. Then you drop them off at a national toy drive location. Have someone take a photo of you donating the toys. The same goes for collecting and donating clothing, both new and gently used.

Nursing Home

Collect safe unbreakable prizes for bingo in a nursing home. Collect gently used sweaters, wraps or shawls.

Homeless shelter

Collect shampoo, soap, razors and combs for homeless shelters- clothes for disaster victims.

Lower Income Schools

Collect school supplies, new or gently used uniforms, or school clothing. School uniforms, gently worn or new. Students come in all sizes. Adult clothing is sometimes easier to collect and still looks new. These are good for high school students. Some children outgrow clothing quickly and they still look fresh. Sometimes people are tired of a style or fit and it still meets dress code standard. More schools are going towards the dress code uniform of plain pants, jeans, colored knit shirts, solid sweaters or sweat shirts. Ask the dress code of the schools you want to donate.

Example

White, red or blue polo style shirt with no logo plain slacks, khaki, navy or black.

Prom Donations

Prom formals and jewelry. Check with a lower income school and see if they would like some clothes for prom or other formals. The school's counselor or principal may be a good place to start asking. You can collect clothes to donate to lower income schools for proms and formals. Most bridesmaids are dying to get rid of a dress and shoes that they wore in a wedding. Donations of formals, bridesmaid dresses or dressy cloths for lower income high school. These include jackets, shawls, wraps, crowns, hats or headpieces. This can also include costume jewelry and purses. Take photos for the newspaper or call the TV news and see if a reported wants to cover your story. Do not embarrass the school or place of donation if they do not want it publicized on the news.

Lower Income Pregnancy Clinic

Used maternity clothes and baby clothes. See if you can put up a flyer at some clinics.

Suits & professional work clothes

Collect clothes for people of lower income or out of the workforce. A suit or profession clothing will give a sense of confidence to people when they interview. This will help them with a job and a start on a new life. Many places will be willing to accept these donations. Check and see if your town has a workforce for lower income, prisons, or lower income housing that is willing to accept professional clothing. Ask for donations of suits or professional work cloths and simple costume jewelry, the classics, chain or pearls for women in need at shelters or just out of prison.

Note

Do not reject an item donated to you because it is stained or worn. This can hurt the feeling of the person donating. These items can be disposed discretely. Have receipt stating the cause and date and sign it.

Fun runs, walks or bikes rides

It is easy to participate in an organized charity event. Volunteer on a national level, individually or as a group. Volunteer to be the team leader.

If you have a family member or dear friend with an illness that matches a charity event, choose that cause. Later when you write a scholarship or college entrance essay, you can write about your inspiration to volunteer for a particular cause because of an influential person in your life. They will easily tie together.

If a walk, run or bike ride comes when you have some free time, this is a good time to actively participate. Try to organize a group that you participate with to gather pledges and be a team for the event.

Another idea is to ask friends and family to be on a team. This is a short commitment. Volunteer to be the team captain. To help publicize it, have the team choose a cute, catchy name or decide on a heart-tugging person to honor. Also go to a craft store or a cheap print shop and purchase t-shirts that match. Have a team name printed on one side. If the budget allows, print a photo of the loved one you are doing this in honoring on the shirt. You could include the person's name in the team name, for example "Lisa's Run," or "Angela's Angels."

If the event wants you in their t-shirts, wear matching hats, scarves, sunglasses, Hawaiian leis or something that sets you apart. Take a group photo and submit it to newspapers with team members' names identified under the photo.

Phone Telethons

Many organizations raise money by having a phone drive on television or a radio station. National organizations need volunteers. It looks good on your resume to volunteer for these types of events.

Volunteering makes you feel good about yourself. It makes you feel more confident and opens you up to new experiences. You might make some friends along the way. It gives scholarship judges and college admission representatives a chance to see another side of you.

Start to Finish Example

Let's say you will be collecting used books for soldiers. First, do you have to ship them overseas or are they for a local post? If shipping cannot be donated (a military ship) then maybe there is a veteran hospital or military post in or near your town. Say you live in a city near a military post and you can convince some adult to drive and deliver the items. First, see if the base will be willing to accept the donation. Ask if they have a library or social director. Talk to them and see if they will welcome the donation and when they will be available to accept your contribution. If they say yes, send them a letter confirming your proposal. Show your request and acceptance letter to the place that you want to leave donation box. If they said no, you have not wasted your time writing a plan. If accepted, write a plan timeline showing when you will drop off the boxes and when you will pick them up. Places to leave the donation boxes are places of worship, parent's job locations and school. See if you can have a donation spot for students or even just the teachers' lounge. A good time period for this is 3 weeks.

Get some large boxes that are strong enough to hold the weight. Cover them and make them colorful. This can be with something that is sturdy and will hold up so the boxes look fresh. Cheap fabric or vinyl table cloths will work or you can glue photos from magazines or glue pieces of wrapping paper to the box. This way it will not tear. Now you have nice donation boxes. Make a sign. The less said the better. Used Books for Soldiers at (Name of Base or Hospital). Agree to collect the boxes several times if necessary. Have a plan at home on where you will store the books. When you get the books count each book so you have a number count and also thin out any torn or inappropriate books. Let your family, neighbors, friends, your clubs, and your parents clubs and workplace know of your donation.

Collect all the used books and dress nicely on the day of the donation. If you drive, take a friend. Have your friend or driver take several photos of you in front of the post sign holding a stack of books or a box of books. This is a staged photo. The ideal photo will be of you shaking hands with the person accepting the books. In case they will not take the photo with you use a photo that has already been taken as a backup.

Clean up the area at home or area you stored the books. Send out thank you notes to the people that let you have collection boxes. Contact the local newspaper, the military post papers and if you parents have an office paper or magazine and submit the best photo of you with the book drive and see if they will publish it in their paper.

CHAPTER 7 COLLECTING REFERENCES

Start collecting books to help give you ideas for essay questions, answers to questions on applications or just to have ideas fresh in your memory when questioned in a one on one interview. Garage sales, used books sales, and discount book stores are good places to look for these books.

Types of books

- Pyramid scheme businesses. Look for ones that have personal stories on people that got rich quick, great stories on how they reached and achieved their dreams.

- Religious books and inspirational

- Motivation books

- Books of quotes

- Speech writing

- Essays that work

- You graduated books.

- Diet books that are inspirational

- Time management books

- Letter writing books

- Etiquette or manners books

- Resume books- go through these books and pick words that describe you and work them into your resume or essays. Pull powerful words.

How to use a resume book

Some how to write a resume books have a list of key words. Use these words to describe an event or events you organized. Good words are: determined, initiated, launched, presided, directed, and promoted.

Do not ever plagiarize or copy from a book without using a quote. Computers can catch this and it is wrong to copy. Use these books to inspire you. Use the book as a guide. Use a highlight pen and mark sections in the book that are useful. Put bookmarks in sections that you want to reference.

CHAPTER 8 CORROSPONDING WITH PEOPLE

There will be many thank you notes and correspondences. Keep copies of all letters you send out. You can copy your own letter and change the name of the university and awards. Make sure you proofread and do not send out the wrong letter to a university or person. Do not thank Duke for the visit to Ohio State.

First type the note on a computer. Use spell check and grammar check. You can hand copy the note. Keep the typed note on file and note copies by hand. While handwritten thank you notes are best, if your handwriting is poor type the note on nice plain stationary and sign your signature. Type all correspondence letters.

College

Some colleges keep records of how often you have corresponded with them. If two students are equally qualified they will most likely choose the student that has shown the most interest. If you are going to visit a college, try and make an appointment with the department head to tour the department. Many times the college has a welcome weekend for high school students to visit. If they have a student that they pair you with or an overnight in the dorm get their name and address. Send them a thank you note. These students may be part of the judging process. Keep a record of all correspondences that you have written, whom they were sent to and when they were sent.

Thank You Notes

Buy tasteful thank you notes and plain but nice stationery. A simple Thank You on the top front of the note will do. Stationery can have your name or initials but not silly designs. Office supply stores have some good stationary. Some photocopy shops sell paper by the sheet and envelopes individually. A pale cream, white or gray with little grain or linen texture or is good. Do not sign you name with a happy face design beside it or hearts. As soon as information is sent to you, send a handwritten thank you note to the person that sent the information. If you visit for a weekend send a thank you note to the event coordinator. If you meet with a person in the department you want to pursue, send them a note. A short note written sooner is better than a longer note later. Try and include something personal that you enjoyed or appreciated about the university. Compliment the university on something they are proud.

Example

I was impressed with the science lab, computer lab, library, beautiful grounds, high ranking college reviews, and the prize professor.

Keep a list of all correspondences by university and the name of the person that you sent it to and the date. Keep a copy of the letter you sent on file.

Keep your stamps simple, a flag or something similar. Do not use stamps supporting controversial causes.

Remember to let the college Financial Aid office to know of outside awards.

CHAPTER 9 LISTING GOOD REFERANCES

Teachers

Chose a teacher that likes you. Note: English teacher know how to write GREAT letters.

Counselor

Meet with your counselor at the beginning of the year to discuss you college plans before it get too crazy.

Principal

If you are on good terms meet with the principal.

Club sponsor

Scout leader

Employers

Coaches

Clergy or leader at place of worship

Community leaders

Congressman – Senator- Politician that knows you

An adult at an organization or a charity that you have volunteered at

Never a relative

Example

Food bank leader, pet shelter manager, nursing home manager if you have done volunteer work there and they know you.

Trying to decide which political candidate to volunteer to work with? Is one an alumnus of a university that you want to attend? Volunteer for that candidate. A letter from former alumni will carry more weight with the university. Try and volunteer for a winner but do not volunteer for someone that strongly goes against your views. It is rare to find a political leader that matches all your political views.

When requesting a letter

Give 3 weeks for the letter writer.

Let them know what the letter is for and what information you want included in the letter.

Address of where to mail letter and stamp.

Organize a packet to give to people writing letters of recommendation for you

Include:

Transcript

Resume

Volunteer hours

Letters of praise from others (thanks for organizing fun run team)

Your name addresses and phone number

Copies of newspaper clippings

Address of where to mail letter and stamp or envelope if the organization sent you one

A hint- if the letter is for a volunteer scholarship, list or give information on a project that you have done and want included.

For a leadership scholarship: list organizations that you are a leader.

Always follow up with a thank you note to the person that wrote you a letter of recommendation.

CHAPTER 10 WRITING A STRONG RESUME

Check the current books for the most popular resume style. Right now bullets are popular.

Form for resume. Note change the clubs and organizations to reflect where you have volunteered. This is just an example. If styles change and this looks dated change to what is current.

NAME

Address	phone number
City, State zip	e-mail
GPA: score on a scale of 4.0	SAT xxxx Math xxx Verbal xxx
Class Rank xxx of xxx	*ACT or whatever other test*

CAREER OBJECTIVES Financial advisor with a double bachelor's degree in Accounting and Marketing with a master's degree in similar field.

HIGH SCHOOL   *school name* High School

       Address

       City

       School phone number

       Name of School District

ADVANCED PLACEMENT CLASSES list classes here

<u>COMMUNITY SERVICE AND ACTIVITIES</u>

- <u>Program</u> title if any.   Years served

  Description of job duty

  Good words: managing- voting- member- recruited – initiated- fundraiser

  representative -managed- promoted- collected and delivered

  List amount of money (if a large amount), books collected, people served,

  people managed

- <u>Church Council</u> Youth Representative. year -year

  Voting member on church council.

- <u>Church Property Committee</u> year-year

  Managing of property and building.

- <u>State Youth Outdoor Program</u> with Texas Parks and Wildlife. Assistant.

  Exhibitor at trade shows. Worked to introduce youths to educational

  wildlife experiences and recruit landowners for donations of land use

  year-year

- <u>Distributive Education Club of America</u> member year-year Vice President. Marketing work-study program District Conference Finalist DECA State Conference Participant

- <u>Veteran Hospital Book Drive</u>. Initiated used books for Veteran Hospital, promoted, collected and delivered to hospital. Donated about 450 books. year

CHAPTER 11 RECORDING ALL VOLENTEER WORK

Record all your volunteer work. Write your hours in decimals. Record the date, volunteer group, and work done. Adding fractions involves converting while decimals add quickly on excel or a calculator. Round to the nearest quarter hour.

You will have 2 logs, one by calendar year- the month and day, and a separate one divided by organizations that you do most of your volunteer work. Have a miscellaneous log for other volunteer work. Both should add up to the same amount.

Hours are recorded on the left side so it is easier to add.

Keep a separate chapter in each log for your school year.

Remember to keep track of you hours so you do not have to play catch up to get around 300 volunteer hours in 4 years.

Example: Pat is planning a busy spring and will be in a spring theater group and taking spring SAT test. Pat will not available to do much volunteer work in the spring.

Because of this Pat is volunteering for the following in the fall:

- Elected position- church council youth representative- meets once a month.

- SPCA pet shelter showing dogs in a pet store for adoption. Pat made a six-week commitment to show adoptable animals.

- Book drive- independently with the books going to a veteran hospital.

Lots of hours will be recorded this 3-month period. If Pat takes time off from volunteering in the spring her volunteer hours will be on track. There are times in your life when hours for volunteering are easier. When you can make spare time it would be a good to look into doing short-term volunteer projects. That way you will have stored away hours for times that you have other obligations.

Example of Pat's volunteer log:

By calendar all in date order

Month Year
Hour date work done <u>organization</u>

Hour date work done <u>organization</u>

Hour date work done <u>organization</u>

September

1.75 Sept 4 business meeting <u>Church Council</u>

2.5 Sept 8 showed pets for adoption <u>SPCA</u>

1.5   Sept 10 wrote book drive proposal <u>Book Drive</u>

.75   Sept 12 Contacted VA hospital about book donations <u>Book Drive</u>

2.5   Sept 15 showed pets for adoption <u>SPCA</u>

3   Sept 15 shopped- boxes <u>Book Drive</u>

1   Sept 16 request for books church <u>Book Drive</u>

2   Sept 18 called family and friends requesting book donations <u>Book Drive</u>

2.5   Sept 22 showed pets for adoption <u>SPCA</u>

2.5   Sept 29 showed pets for adoption <u>SPCA</u>

<u>Oct</u>

3   Oct 5 collected boxes from offices counted and sorted
books <u>Book Drive</u>

2.5   Oct 6 showed pets for adoption <u>SPCA</u>

1.5 Oct 9 business meeting <u>Church</u> <u>Council</u>

0.5   Oct10 called VA hospital for delivery of books <u>Book Drive</u>

2.5   Oct 13 showed pets for adoption <u>SPCA</u>

1. Oct 13 loaded and delivered books to VA hospital <u>Book Drive</u>

2.5   Oct 20 showed pets for adoption <u>SPCA</u>

2.5   Oct 27 showed pets for adoption <u>SPCA</u>

<u>November</u>

2.5   Nov 3 showed pets for adoption <u>SPCA</u>

2 Nov 6 Church business <u>Church Council</u>

2.5 Nov 10 showed pets for adoption <u>SPCA</u>

2.5 Nov 17 showed pets for adoption <u>SPCA</u>

ORGANIZED BY EVENT OR CHARITY

Church Council

1.75 <u>Sept 4 business meeting</u>

1.5 <u>Oct 9 business meeting</u>

5.25 Nov 6 Church business

SPCA

2.5 Sept 8 showed pets for adoption

2.5 Sept 15 showed pets for adoption

2.5 Sept 22 showed pets for adoption

2.5 Sept 29 showed pets for adoption

2.5 Oct 6 showed pets for adoption

2.5 Oct 13 showed pets for adoption

2.5 Oct 20 showed pets for adoption

2.5 Oct 27 showed pets for adoption

2.5 Nov 3 showed pets for adoption

2.5 Nov 10 showed pets for adoption

2.5 Nov 17 showed pets for adoption

Book Drive

1.5   Sept 10 wrote book drive proposal

0.75   Sept 12 Contacted VA hospital about book donations

2   Sept 15 shopped made boxes and posters for book collection

1   Sept 16 request for books church

2   Sept 18 called family and friends requesting book donations

2   Oct 5 collected boxes from offices counted and sorted books

0.5   Oct10 called VA hospital for delivery of books

3.5   Oct 13 loaded and delivered books to VA hospital

Separate by Organizations

When you separate your volunteer hours by organizations do a separate section for each school calendar year, one each for your Freshman, Sophomore, Junior and Senior year. Count the summer before class begins to the end of the class term as one academic calendar year. If you have year round classes, determine the calendar year ending when you get promoted to the next grade. If school starts in August and ends in May in your district

Freshman   June 2016 -May 2017

Sophomore   June 2017- May 2018

Get signed volunteer work

Say you volunteered numerous Saturday mornings for two and a half hours for a pet shelter. They show animals up for adoption at a local pet store. You now have made contact with the pet shelter manager and the manager of the pet store. Now you have 2 people that may be a good choice for a letter of recommendation.

Take a photo of you with the pets if you can. This can be handy later.

Separate and print out organizations and have someone sign off the volunteered hours. For example, if you do volunteer work at a church have the church representative sign off on your church volunteer work. If you did work at an animal shelter have the animal shelter manager sign on your volunteer work.

Before you volunteer, let the organization leader or manager know that colleges want you to keep track of your volunteer hours. Let them know college and scholarship forms often they ask for number of volunteer hours or community service hours. If necessary, let them know you are not doing the work as part of a court-ordered sentence by a judge. Ask them nicely if they would sign an informal paper stating your volunteer hours. If they have a form, even better. Still keep track of your hours anyway. If not, let them know you would be glad to keep track of your hours and print out a letter for them to review and sign. Another reason to get your volunteer hours signed often is in case there is a dispute about the work you are doing, you will know before you commit too many hours for that organization.

Print out your volunteer work by organization and put your name at the top of the list. Type the name and title of the person that you report to for the organization or bottom of the page. Ask them to sign the list to verify that you have volunteered those hours. Have the volunteer hours signed every couple of months or when there is a change of whoever is in charge.

Example

The animal shelter is changing managers. Have the old manager sign the hours you have done for them. Start a new time list when the new manager starts and then the new manager can sign the hours you have done after they have started working there.

When filling out scholarships note "signed volunteer hours" so they know you did not make it up. Some volunteer work is just easier. What is easiest to each person depends on their likes or dislikes. Some people find walking the neighborhood collecting books from people they know relaxing while others would prefer showing off animals for an adoption.

Note

Some things rack up volunteer hours really quickly

Being a camp counselor for a weekend retreat linked to a charitable cause can be as much as 48 hours or more. Doing a fundraiser show for a fee that is donated to a charitable cause can count rehearsal hours.

Garage sale or silent auction, count collecting time, organizing, pricing, setting up and cleaning up. This could get 12 hours or more very easily.

CHAPTER 12 DRESSING FOR SUCCESS

Dress: What to wear for an interview or college visit

Make sure your clothes are not wrinkled. Iron, if necessary and make sure your clothes are clean. Do not wear something brand new that might have a tag that scratches you. Give the clothes you plan to wear a test try on. Do not wear anything too fussy or has a busy print. If you are not sure of your outfit have a friend take your picture front, back and sides of the outfit that you chose to wear. See how you look in the outfit from all four sides in the outfit that you are wearing to the interview.

Note

If going to interview that you know will be serving BBQ or pasta supper or any dish that is saucy or messy, wear a print that will hide any food spills.

For Ladies and Men

Nails, Trim nails neat & clean

Light on perfume or cologne, or no cologne.

No visible tattoos.

Fresh breath. Have breath mints or gum but be through with it when you enter.

Nothing in your mouth, mints or gum when interviewing.

Have a comb or brush.

Shoes neat and clean. No clogs or flip-flops or sandals.

No baseball caps or hats or head covering – except required by religion.

Red can come across as to powerful; use carefully.

Be careful with black. Black can be tasteful or look Goth. You know the difference.

No pins except flag or religious if going to a religious university.

A lapel pin is acceptable if it is a non-controversial cause that you supported. Pins supporting diabetes or heart awareness.

Carry an attaché or folder, some have fabric or leather finish, to hold your resume or and papers that you want to take to your interview. Make sure it is fresh and clean. Keep it a simple black, brown or neutral color unless you are going for an art or similarly creative degree.

Men

Shirt, belt, tie, pants without cargo pockets. Safe shirt colors are white, light blue, light gray or cream. Men, learn how to tie a necktie. If you cannot learn to tie a neck tie find a good quality clip on tie. Clean shaven or neat and trim facial hair. No earrings or necklaces. Keep on any medical alert jewelry. Remove earrings and or necklace unless going to a liberal art college. Rings: one ring, two are acceptable if not too loud or flashy.

Ladies

Light on the makeup. No spike heels or very casual sandals. If wearing earrings, hoop earrings the size of quarter or smaller or simple earrings. No more than 1 ring on each hand unless it is a combo ring. Avoid pockets over the chest No fishnet hose or similar printed hose. Do not wear a bow in hair or hair jewelry. Exception is a bow on a ponytail with your hair pulled back. Keep the bow small. Make sure the first thing people see is you and not a bow. Wear the ponytail low. No ponytails to the side or on the top of the head. Never wear pig tails. If you have long hair and going to an evening event a ponytail with a tasteful ponytail holder is acceptable. Jeweled is ok if going to an evening event. It is better to be on time than late from doing your hair. Do not wear loud jewelry that makes noise like charm bracelets or a stack of hoop bracelets that make noise when you move. If at a meal, do not wear jewelry that can fall into your food if you lean forward while eating. An example is a long pendant or beads that move when you lean forward. Cover your mid section No cleavage. Do not wear too many pieces of jewelry such as pins, necklaces, and bracelets. When sitting without coverage such as a chair in the open; keep legs together in a short skirt. Do not wear too short of a skirt or any clothes that are going to cause a problem. Example: wrap around skirt, a wrap around dress that is not secure. Polish clear or light clear pink tint or French manicure. Keep nails medium to short. No long nails, no press on decals or nail jewelry. Do not wear pink or light purple. No ruffles. Try to avoid looking too girly. Take a good look at your outfit and make sure it is not too matronly. Is this something that a senior citizen would wear?

Arriving at an Interview

Be 10 minutes early to interview. Do not come too early. If you arrive too early, find a place nearby to stay. Have clear directions even if it is on campus. Make sure you know the building with a campus map. Do a trial run to find it if necessary. Have their phone number in case you are lost or delayed which should not happen since you have done a trial run. There could be an emergency that is unavoidable. Have a pen. Have two or more resumes. One to offer and one to read along. A third may be nice if you have two people interview you. Have a sheet with phone numbers and addresses of your school, employers, your parent's employers, personal references and volunteer contacts.

CHAPTER 13 PHOTOGRAPHING YOURSELF

Follow the same rules as dressing for an interview but keep all the lines simpler and avoid busy prints. Make sure clothes fit right and do not bunch on your shoulders. When you sit for the photos make sure you clothes are still in the proper place. Jackets can rise up above the shoulders when sitting and not lay flat on your shoulder. A model tip is to take clothespins. If you have excess fabric when poising for your photo tighten, but not too tight, the back with a clothespin. Make sure clothes are not too tight or too revealing. A discount store photographer can often get photos as good as an expensive studio. Keep the background simple like a solid light or soft color. Do not use their fall foliage or winter wonderland background. Do not use props unless it is an instrument that you play and you are going for a music scholarship. A laptop does not work if you are going for a business degree. A good rule is does this photograph look acceptable to give your stuffiest family member.

Candid photos

On applications you can try and include a photo of you on one of your charitable events. Make sure nothing is growing behind your head (standing in front of a pole or centerpiece) and your hands are in a safe place.

Example

Donating to a charitable event, managing a charity fund event. Running or walking for an event. Being a team leader is a bonus. These are great photos to try to place in your local newspaper or office paper,

CHAPTER 14 MINDING YOUR MANNERS

Manners book

Get a simple elementary manner book and review it before an interview. These are quick to read and cover the basics. Be on guard on the phone. Let your friends and family know that you will be out of contact during the interview process and will contact them when you can. Silence all devices on your phone and ask them to not call you during your interviews. Be on guard when making a phone call in a public place. Remember anything said in the restroom can be heard and judged. You do not know who else is in the room overhearing your conversation. If must contact someone text.

Please and thank you

Always send a thank you note. Reply if the invitations ask please reply or RSVP which means the same thing.

Meals

Many interviews involve a meal. Always let the host or hostess starts eating first unless they insist you start. . Learn which fork to use. Wait until the host or hosts starts eating and follow what they do. If there is a menu, ask what they suggest. Do not order the most expensive item or cheapest. Take a cue from your host and order something in a similar price range. Do not order pasta with sauces that may be messy or soups unless you have no other choice. In some cases, it will be a catered menu and go along with the meal unless you have religious or moral objections to the food. Now is not the time to preach on the treatment of veal.

Discretely ask if another choice is available. If the restaurant is fancier than anything you have ever seen try and look like you fit in with everyone. You can comment on how nice the restaurant is but do not look like you do not fit in at events above your social level scale. College is a time to grow and learn.

Do not take any phone calls during a meal or text during a meal. You can leave your phone on silent and if there is a serious problem excuse yourself to the restroom and then check. By serious someone should be in an extreme emergency to contact you such as a medical family emergency. If there is a meal do not let your guard down. You are being judged from the moment they see you until you leave the parking lot. In fact, be polite to the parking attendant if there is one. While current events are good to discuss follow the conversation that the host is leading. Also do not discuss anything gross at the dinner table even if it flows into the conversation. If an illness or death is the answer to a question do not give gory details during a meal. Check the news and a current event magazine so you know what is going on in the world.

Do not over rehearse

Remember that this may be the university's first visual impression of you. To be invited to an interview means that you have already made a good impression on paper. Be yourself, relax and enjoy the process. Do not be so relaxed that you are not always composed. This is not the time to share too much, but enough that they learn about you. If you are nervous, take three deep breaths without looking like you are huffing and puffing. Look relaxed even if you are faking it. Smile. If

you are nervous or scared do not let it show.

CHAPTER 15 ACHIEVING A STRONG TRANSCRIPT

Make sure you are taking all the classes required for entrance at the university that you want to attend. Check out which classes are required for the university. Take extra classes in your field that you want a degree.

Math- Mathematical classes and statistics

Medical- Science or psychology

Business- Check business courses at your school Public speaking- Unless you think your grade will be so low it would affect your GPA a public speaking class can come in handy in life. Save all report cards as back up.

CHAPTER 16 APPLYING FOR SCHOLARSHIP & COLLEGE

Make sure you qualify for a scholarship or university before you apply. Photocopy all scholarship forms. Highlight on your extra copy all the things they want you to send to them. Example: Transcript, SAT score, letter of recommendation, essay. Fill out the information on the photocopy. Proof read it a day later or after a break and see if the answers make sense and look correct. Photocopy all application forms. Even if you have to hand write on the application form, type the answers on a computer and do spell check. Make sure all spelling and grammar are correct. Only then do you copy your answer on the scholarship form. Make sure the application is neat. For an essay requested on a scholarship or college entrance application run spell and grammar check. Ask a teacher you trust or someone with excellent grammar and spelling to proofread you essay. Ask them to note anything that they cannot follow or that they find confusing.

If financial need is a requirement in the scholarship and you are not in a financially needy family, do not waste your time applying.

Are you meeting the deadline?

Include all information that they ask. Answer all questions. Questions on volunteer leadership and community service are often included on scholarships. This is where your years of documented work are used. Your book will help you be ahead of others trying to figure out what they did. Scholarship judges are looking for more than volunteer work required for scouts, or honor society or other organizations. They are looking for leadership; self initiate volunteer work and holding titles in clubs or organizations. Now is the time to brag about any awards or honors you have received. If you have had a hardship or obstacle in your life, there may be a question on what you did to overcome adversity and succeed

Example

Parent had cancer. I helped around the house, gave rides for chemo, and lead a 5K run team for cancer.

Example

English was my second language. I started a tutorial program to help student non-English speakers learn English. Parent was sent overseas in military I did a book drive for a VA hospital or started an email pen pal a soldier and "adopt a soldier" in my community (Community can be any relatives you can talk into helpings, your school, neighbors, place of worship and anyone else)

CHAPTER 17 IMPROVING YOUR NTERVIEW SKILLS

Check chapter 12 on how to dress. Do not wear anything uncomfortable. Check the university brochures to get an idea on how dressy or casual the college is. In some universities a suit is needed for men, others a shirt and tie while others a shirt and slacks. Now is not a time to express you individuality or fun T-shirt collection. Be on guard from time you enter parking lot or building. Read your resume and awards to remind yourself of all the wonderful things about you. If it is cold outside and you are inside take you coat off. Try and get settled after you enter the building but before you enter the interviewing room. A restroom is a good place to check your hair, clothes, make-up. Have a breath mint. Finish it before entering the interview room. Do not chew gum or candy while interviewing. If you are a smoker (not advised) do not smoke before the interview. You may not smell the smoke, but others can. Offer a handshake and look them in the eye. Say "nice to meet you" or "pleased to meet you" and say their name if it seem natural. Have an attaché case or bag with your resume, phone numbers and addresses of your school, employers, references and anyone else you think you might need. Have it easy to find so you are not rummaging in a bag. If you think it would help, get bright colored folders to put your papers in. Put the folder in your case where it will be easy to reach. You can color code for your resume and use another color for references.

Before the interview

If you can, video or record questions and answers with a friend and play it back to see how you sound. Make your answers sound fresh and not rehearsed. While you can plan an answer do not have the answers memorized line for line. If the answer to a question should be a deep thoughtful answer and you immediately know the answer look like you are thinking and silently count to three, then answer the question.

Have answers for basic questions

What have you done that makes you proud?

Some accomplishment, volunteer work that you have done, an award you won science project or 1st chair in orchestra or sports accomplishment.

Where are you from?

Have something nice to say about your town or state even if you want to leave and never return. You hometown has a great climate, near a beautiful lake, famous or interesting founder of city, sports team, any history or growth.

What do you want to be?

Have a career idea. If you do not have a career idea say you have several ideas in mind. You enjoy (whatever, say photography or sports) and want to peruse career options in that direction.

Where do you picture yourself in 10 years?

Good answers are working in (whatever) field, playing in a symphony, doing research, writing a book, and teaching, starting a charity or private practice. In a fulfilling career in (the field that my degree is in) such as teaching, nursing, or banking. Starting a program for (whatever your interest is) Researching (whatever) Holding a public office. Poor example: Married, pregnant, rich, retired. The wrong answer is married and with children. Have a career goal. .
Be positive and upbeat without looking too perky or goofy.

What challenge have you overcome?

If your life is sunny still have an answer. Scheduling your study time with your charitable activities is a good answer. If you have had something serious mention that. Helping out while my parent had a medical problem, overcoming shyness, learning English. Exception: You do not have to share you everything. If you have overcome something personal that you do not want to share do not share the information, especially if it can be held against you. .

Have a question planned about the university. It can be about the school's history, schools growth, the city the school is in, or the field of your interest. Check the newspaper or a news web site for current events or most popular on Internet or watch the national news on TV. Have some opinion on hot topics. Also check out some social or gossip magazine in case they ask a popular current event question. . Do not get too extreme with your opinions. .

Interview

Look like you are interested. Do not fidget, twirl hair, jingle change, or chew gum. Have your cell phone off. Do not twirl your rings or pull at any jewelry or your clothes.

If you need to force interest look at the person that is interviewing you eyebrows, count their freckles, crow's feet or hair. There is something about almost anyone that can give you something to look at.

If you do not have an answer say I will get back to you. It is better than making up something stupid. If you belong to an organization that has letters or a strange name know what it stands. Example: CROP Walk . The letters do not stand for anything. The word crop means food grown from a crop. The organization started from farmers giving food from their crop to the needy.

Be prepared to answer these questions or statements

Describe yourself

This does not mean to be bluntly honest or share family skeletons. Describe your interests, dreams, and goals.

<u>Why did you choose this college?</u>

Say something they want to hear. The rich history of the university, the academics, or the small class size. They do not want to hear that they are offering the most money. This may be true but do not tell them this. Keep your answers brief but make sure you describe why you are the best choice. If they want more information they will ask. Do not let your voice rise and get squeaky. Do not give more information than asked. When asked about your family, do not share information about cousins or distant relatives unless they went to the university or inspired you to your career choice. Somewhere in the interview let them know you really, really want this scholarship and are qualified. Let them know why you fit the match. Do not beg. If you do not know what they are asking ask them to clarify the question.

Have a question or two ready to ask them about the university or the program or town. At the end of the interview thank the person for their time and consideration. "Thank you for your time and consideration "Offer to shake hands again if it seems appropriate. Get their card if they have one. If they do not have a card when you leave find out their address.

Send a thank you card

Send a thank you card to your interviewer promptly but do not put it in the out box as you are leaving the interview.

CHAPTER 18 KEEPING YOUR RECORD CLEAN

It goes without saying but I will say it anyway. Do not steal. Do not drink or get caught drinking. Do not get arrested for anything, even stupid stuff. If your friends are having fun doing stupid criminal mischief think of how much more fun you will have with a high paying job and the money to do what you want such as a travel, a nice home, a boat, or a fine car. In fact, if your friends are that stupid make new friends. Do not do drugs. Do not post photos or write anything on the internet that can come back and haunt you. Companies have been known to check internet sites to review candidates. Some schools ask you to open you social internet sites. Make sure your links do not reveal something questionable about you. Do not get pregnant or get someone pregnant. Starting a family does not make it easier to get a degree. If you have a child, get a good education. This can be an essay topic on challenges that caused responsibility and maturity.

CHAPTER 19 EXAMPLE OF LETTERS – ESSAYS- APPLICATIONS

On any official officer holder use the following form.

HOW TO ADDRESS YOUR LEGISLATORS

TITLE	ADDRESS	SALUTATION
President of the United States	The President The White House Washington, D.C. 20500	Sir Mr. President Dear Mr. President
U.S. Senator	The Honorable _____ United States Senate Washington, D.C. 20510	Sir Dear Senator
Congressman / Congresswoman	The Honorable _____ U.S. House of Representatives	Sir / Madame Dear Congressman Congresswoman
State Senator	The Honorable _____ State Senator Legislative Office Building Albany, N.Y. 12247	Sir / Madame Dear Senator
State Assemblyman / Assemblywoman	The Honorable _____ Assemblyman / woman	Sir / Madame Dear Assemblyman / Assemblywoman
Governor	The Honorable _____ Governor, State of New York Executive Chamber State Capital Albany, N.Y. 12224	Dear Governor
Mayor	His / Her Honor The Mayor	Dear Mayor
County Executive	Mr. / Ms. _____ County Executive Address	Dear Mr. / Ms.
County Legislator	The Honorable _____ Address	Dear Mr. / Ms.
Councilman / Councilwoman	Councilman / Councilwoman Address	Dear Councilman / Councilwoman

Letter to a congressman or senator requesting nomination to a US military academy

Note: All the paper work for Naval Academy, Air Force Academy and West Point needs to be completed before October. Please check and see if this date has changed.

Date

Honorable **Name**
Their Address Street
Their City, State, zip code

Dear Senator or Congressman **Name**,

It is my desire to attend the **United States Naval Academy or other academy**. I would like to be considered as one of your nominees for the class entering in the summer of (year). I look forward to serving my country.

My pertinent data:

Your name

Social Security #: **Number**

Name of Parents: **name of both parents father's name mother's name- if single parent their name only**

City, State zip code

Mailing: **Home Address Street**

City, State zip code

Telephone: **Phone number home**

Phone number cell

Date of Birth: **Month day year**

Place of Birth: **City State Country if not USA**

High School Attended: **Name of school High School- Name of   School District**

Date of High School Graduation: **Month Year**

My approximate standing is **your class number** in a class of graduation **class size**

Results of my ACT and/or ATP (SAT-I) test scores are: ***not in yet or test scores***

High School extracurricular activities: see attached

Thank you for considering my request for one of your nominations.

Sincerely yours,

Your signature

Request for a sponsor of a project

Example of a real letter

Date

Dear Name,

I am trying to be founder of a fundraiser for the Veterans Hospital. I have spoken with Dana at the V.A. hospital and would like to initiate a used-book drive at the school, my church, and see if my office would allow a box in the break room (if you think it would be a good idea to ask). I would like to leave a box at the teachers' break room at the school and the other high school locations, if they will let me. I would like the collection to be three weeks in October, before the Christmas drives start. I will cover the box and label it used books for VA Hospital. I will empty the boxes at each location as it becomes necessary. I would like to make the donation to the veteran's hospital around Veterans Day.

There are many hospitalized veterans. Some can be long term patients. Reading is a pleasant way to escape. There are veteran extended care homes that would also appreciate used books.

I was wondering if you could be my school sponsor for this project. I will do all the dropping off of boxes and collecting of books and taking them to the Veteran Hospital. I would like to have help getting approval with the school and documenting my volunteer hours. I will keep a chart. I am trying to combine reading and volunteering and give back to the veterans that have given so much to us.

Feel free to contact me if you need any more information.

Sincerely,

 Signature

Typed name

Note

 If you are collecting items in a box cover the box and make it look nice. You can use gift wrapping paper, cheap table cloths, cheap shower curtains or fabric.

<u>Request for a sponsor of a project</u>

Make it your own

Date

Dear Name,

I am trying to be founder of a fundraiser for the

What is you cause

 I have spoken with

Name at location

I would like to initiate a

What do you want to do and what are you collecting

 I would like to leave a box at

Where do you want a collection site or how do you want to collect

I would like the collection to be

Dates of collection drive- usually 3 weeks is a good time line

End date

I will cover the box and label it

What you will label it, books for whatever, clothes, food whatever you are collecting

I will empty the boxes at each location as it becomes necessary. I would like to make the donation to the

Who are you donating to and what date you want to make the donation?

Say something about the need and your cause

I was wondering if you could be my school sponsor for this project. I will do all

the dropping off of boxes and collecting of

Whatever you are collecting

Item you are collecting

Where are you taking them - name of organization and their location?

I would like to have help getting donation approval with the

School, church, office or wherever you are collecting

And documenting my volunteer hours. I will keep a chart. I am trying to combine

volunteering and giving.

Say something nice about your cause

Feel free to contact me if you need any more information.

Sincerely,

Signature

Your name typed

Example of a request for donation

1234 my Street

City, State zip

Date

Dear Mrs. Bush,

I am collecting used books for the Veteran Administration Hospital's library. My name is *your name* and I am *a junior at Name of High School.* I know that you are a firm advocate of reading and President George Bush is a strong supporter of volunteer work. I participate in many group volunteer projects but wanted a project that I initiated alone. I have collected several hundred paper and hardback books. I was wondering if you or your staff had any used books that they would like to donate. I could pick them up at your office, or where ever you chose if you want to participate. Just your and President Bush's inspiration has help me and that is why I decided on a book drive. Being in a hospital can get boring and reading can be a nice diversion.

President George W. Bush is lucky to have a mother like you supporting him.

Sincerely,

Signature

Typed name

Please put you political views aside when contacting a person for a donation. Barbara Bush has strongly supported volunteerism and Laura Bush supports reading.

<u>Requesting a donation – Make it your own</u>

Your street Address

Your city state zip code

Date

Dear Persons name,

I am collecting

What are you collecting?

My name is

 <u>your name</u>

And I am a

 Class rank at Name of School.

Say something nice about them and why you chose them for a donation.

Why you want to do it? My family member, uncle or aunt has diabetes,

cancer or I am concerned about lower income, disaster, veterans.

What you have done so far for the cause?

What do you want from them? An item for a silent auction, books, clothes, recipes for a cook book –physical donations are easier to ask for than money unless it is a donation to a fun run/walk.

Make it easy for them to donate, volunteer to pick up or a meeting place or an address to donate.

Why they inspired you? Are they supporting a similar cause? Does their family member have an illness that you are supporting? Politicians should be interested in most current events, disasters and supporting lower income people to help themselves "I know you understand how important it is for lower income women to have a professional outfit for interview"

*S*incerely,

Your signature

Your name typed

Thank you letter for a donation

Always send a thank you letter for a donation. Offer a receipt when collecting the donation.

Date

Dear name

Thank you for your donation of

State donation

Because of you and others like you

State what you are doing that is wonderful.

Example: We are helping the disaster victims or giving books to lower income children.

Thanks again for you support of my

Whatever you are doing.

Sincerely

Signature

Your name typed

Requesting information from a University

Date

Name of University

My name is **name** and I am interested in information about your university.

I am pursuing a degree in

What are you interested in.

I would like to be a

A job related to your degree.

I will be forwarding test scores to you as I get them.

Please send me some information on your university, including information on your

Department you are interested in, financial aid and

Something about the university that you are interested in. Music program, clubs, season tickets to sports. Try and sound like you are interested in something about their university besides academics and scholarships

Please put me on your mailing list for:

Their open house or they may use a different name for visits

I would also like to know if you have overnight visits.

I look forward to hearing from you in the future. Feel free to call, email or write if you need any more information.

Sincerely,

Signature

Your name typed

Request for a scholarship application

This is an example of a student wanting an accounting or finance degree

Your street address

City, state, zip code

Date

Name of Department Scholarships Committee

Their address

Dear **(Name of Scholarship) Committee Chairperson**,

I am applying to University Name for *a name of* degree. I am presently working as a bank teller and want to continue working in a related industry. I enjoy working with people and helping them build a better future in their investments. My goal is to be in a position to help people with their financial interests. A scholarship would allow me to spend more time studying instead of working to pay my tuition. I am very impressed with *University name* business program. Your high teacher to student ratio will provide a much better education than the large state colleges in *state.* I will be responsible for most of my college expenses. I believe I have a lot to offer your university. I am looking forward to putting my skills in community building leadership and work experience to use in your college.

Very respectfully yours,

Your signature

Your name typed

Request for a scholarship application

How to make it your own

Your street address

City, state, zip code

Date

Name of Department Scholarships Committee

Their address

Dear (Name of Scholarship) Committee Chairperson:

I am applying to University Name for a name of degree. I am presently

What are you doing that will impress them, a job or volunteer work

And want to (or I enjoy)

What do you enjoy about your volunteer work or job that relates to your

future

My goal is to be in a position to

What job do you want, maybe not right now but in a couple of years?

I am very impressed with University name's school program.

What impresses you about the university- the professors, the department, the

schools history

I will be responsible for most of my college expenses, or this helps me with

meeting the cost of my education if there is no way you are responsible for most of

you college expenses. Do not lie if you parents are giving you a full ride.

A scholarship would allow me to spend more time studying than if I had to work

and pay my tuition. I believe I have a lot to offer your university.

I am looking forward to putting my skills in

What skills or talents do you have, leadership, sports, debate, drama,

computer, teaching children

At your university.

Very respectfully yours,

Your signature

Your name typed

Thank you for Scholarship Letter

Date

*Dear (**Name of Scholarship**) Committee Chairperson:*

I am honored to be chosen a recipient of the

Name of Scholarship and name of second scholarship if there is one. Your

generous offer will help make my educational goals attainable. I am seriously

interested in the

Whatever interests you at the university honors program, music, sports

Do not mention that it is a party school, drinking, freedom from parents, act

responsible on paper

I look forward to attending college. Thank you for the distinction you have

given me.

Sincerely,

Your signature

Your name typed

Two Examples of letters accepting scholarships or award

1234 my Street

City, State zip

Date

Dear N*ame,*

I am honored to be chosen a recipient of the *Name of Scholarship* and the

regional scholarship. Your generous offer will make my educational goals

attainable. I am seriously interested in the Honor's College.

I look forward to attending *Name of University*. Thank you for the distinction

you have given me.

Sincerely,

Signature

Typed name

Example 2

34 my Street

City, State zip

Date

Dear *Name*,

I am honored to be chosen the recipient of <u>the name of award</u> .

According to Napoleon "A leader is a dealer in hope."
I have hope for the future of our great country and want to give back in community service. This is why I am walking for food drives, raising money to detonate landmines in Asia and collecting books for our hospitalized veterans.

This award also says to me that someone else believes in me. Thank you for the distinction given to me.

Sincerely,

Signature

Typed name

Turning down a scholarship or admittance

Please take the time to turn down scholarships or admittance slot at universities that you will not attend. This is the responsible thing to do.

Example

Name

Address

Office of Admissions

Name of University

Date

I am writing to thank you for the time and effort you have put into awarding me a scholarship at University Name. This decision has been a difficult one.

After examining several universities and their programs, I have decided to go to

Where are you going? They want to know.

Thank you again for your consideration.

Sincerely,

Signature

Your typed name

Thank you for your reference or recommendation

Date

Thank you for

Writing a letter or filling out a form of recommendation

for me. I appreciate your time and input.

I will keep you posted on my college plans.

Sincerely,

Your name typed

This letter can also be hand written on a nice thank you card.

Essay

An essay usually asks what goals and accomplishments you have achieved and what you overcame. Try and include your volunteer work. Write what you learned from your volunteer or committee work that you can carry in your life. It is alright to brag about yourself. Have someone you trust to proof read the essay to see if they understand what you wrote and have it proof read for spelling and grammar. Use words that you normally use. It is a good idea to have a copy of your resume when you write your essay.

If you were inspired to do something because of a hardship or illness (yours, family or friend) now is the time to bring it up. Did you do something for soldiers or veterans? Was there a family member or friend that was in the service?

An example of an Essay

American Heritage Dictionary defines leadership as the ability to lead and having the capacity to be a leader. From the time I was a child my parents have been involved in organizations as well as our community. Being surrounded in this involvement, I had the opportunity to volunteer in various organizations. Eventually, I found myself taking charge of committees, delegating the work, and taking the responsibility to accomplish the end result in a satisfactory and timely manner.

I was involved in an outdoor program for children and teenagers sponsored by Texas Parks and Wildlife Department called the Texas Outdoor Program. This program provided youths the outdoor opportunities on private land. To further support this group that taught me so much, I participated in a training class. Upon completion of this class, I worked trade shows that allowed me to introduce other youths the opportunity to wildlife and the outdoors while promoting landowners to donate the right to use their property. This activity, along with the training programs, taught me salesmanship and how to motivate people.

Through my church we have always supported the CROP walk. This organization raise funds for worldwide food pantries, shelters, cultivate equipment and deactivating landmines. For 27 years my preacher held the position of our recruiter for our congregation. When he retired from our church I stepped up for the position. As the recruiter, I supported people to walk, challenged pledges, posted announcements, processed consent forms, oversaw collections and deposits, and prepared reports for the organizations. I was in charge of 54 walkers and together we got over $3,000 for our cause. This experience taught me that age did not restrict the ability to lead an activity and the importance of teamwork in accomplishing the objectives.

I personally believe that some veterans are unfairly disregarded in our society. There are many hospitalized veterans, some for the rest of their lives. I decided to initiate a used book drive for the local veterans. I presented a proposal to my church council and contacted the veteran hospital. I wrote publicity articles and motivational speeches that I presented to my congregation, promoted the cause, gathered donations and delivered the books by Veterans Day. The highlight of this endeavor was that Barbara Bush supported my drive by donating a book. This project taught me the importance of a solid proposal. My community made this event a success by the large volumes of donated books.

Assuming a leadership role in these activities has taught me how to work with people and motivate a group to accomplish a goal. I plan to continue helping others during my college years and life. I look forward to seeing how I can be of service at *University name*

Note

This essay stated 3 volunteer activities. One independently organized. It also demonstrates skills learned from the volunteer work .

Public speaking

Writing publicity articles

Writing proposals

Working trade shows

Managing money

CHAPTER 20 LOG –KEEPING TRACK IN A LOGBOOK

CLAENDAR

One Week Rule

Always give yourself a week margin for deadlines. If an application is due on the 14th have it done by the 7th. This will make your life simpler if an emergency comes your way. Many scholarships or college applications are rejected because they do not meet the deadline.

Get a big wall calendar, the one with big squares to write in. Put both the actual deadlines and a notice one week before the deadlines. You may want to color code the boxes by circling the date and writing the information in the box. You may want to color code college deadlines in one color and a different color for scholarships, whatever works for you. Also highlight dates a week in advance to remind whoever is writing a letter or recommendation that they are due on that date.

Keep a back up on whatever personal device, online calendar, or pocket calendar that you keep in your school bag, purse, car or online. Do not trust only one source to store your information.

Example

Call June 1 the person writing a letter of recommendation for scholarship letter of recommendation that had a June 8 postmark deadline. "I am calling to see if you need any information for the letter you are sending to X scholarship for me. I really appreciate you doing this for me". This is nicer than saying did you remember (or forget) to mail in my letter of recommendation.

On the 15 of the month review what is coming up the following month. June 15th check what is ahead in July.

Pick one day of the week and use that day as the day you review what is needed the next seven days.

Keep a back up of all your calendar information in a notebook or computer or other device.

Essay file

Keep a file of all your essays for scholarships. A couple can be reworded for many different universities or scholarships. It is all right to reword you own writings.

Dates

PSAT SAT ACT college placement or other tests

Requested information on college

Wrote thank you notes

Requested information on scholarship

Scholarships to be mailed

College visits

College fairs

College application due dates

Scholarship information due dates

Letter of recommendation due dates

Weekend visits request

Address Book

Keep an address book in your computer or whatever personal device but have a back up copy hand written or type out pages as you go. Your back up can be a cheap spiral notebook. This way if your computer or other device crashes or gets a virus you have a back up copy.

A back up copy can be kept electronically.

Postal Note

Always check with the post office and make sure you have proper postage on any item mailed to universities or scholarship locations.

If you are using one person several times for references it might be a good idea to take that person to lunch or coffee to discuss your future. It will give that person a chance to know you better.

Use the following to keep track of information sent to colleges, universities, and other scholarships. Be sure and check your high school for local scholarships.

General Scholarships Not Related To Universities

Scholarship name

Deadline

Requirements

Request reference letter

Reference letter

Thank you letter for reference

Essay

Transcript if necessary

Universities and Universities Private Scholarships

Repeat each section for a university

University Name

Address

Phone number

Contact name of admissions

 Address

Phone Number

Email

Contact for scholarship

Address

Phone Number

Email

Department head

Address

Phone Number

Email

Department contact

Address

Phone Number

Email

University Name

Requested brochure

E mail thank you or hand written

Send in application

Send in transcript

Request visit

Thank you note for visit

Visit University

Send in SAT-ACT

Requested scholarship application

Request tourism information of college's city or check on the internet. It is good to know a little about the area.

If out of state, get state tourism information.

Request letters of recommendation

Name of reference

Address

Phone Number

Email

Thank you to reference

Name of reference

 Address

Phone Number

Email

Thank you to reference

University Name

Send in scholarship application

Scholarship interview

Contact name

Address

Phone Number

Email

Thank you note to interviewer

Receive scholarship

Grateful thank you note

Housing application or housing

Letter to roommate to coordinate items

Thank you to parents or whoever helped you

Good Luck Archiving your Educational Dreams.

About the Author

Jody Duffey lives in Texas with her husband and 2 labs. She has 2 adult children.

You can contact her at:

prepareforscholarshipmoney@yahoo.com